Oh, The Places You've Been!

Written by Jana Greco
Illustrated by Remi Bryant

All rights reserved. Printed in the United States

No part of this book may be reproduced in any form or by any electronic or mechanical means, including information storage and retrieval systems, without the permission in writing from the author. However, reviewers may quote brief passages in a review.

Copyright © 2020 Jana Greco

ISBN 978-1-954529-11-3

Published by PlayPen Publishing
PlayPenPublishing.com

United States

Dedication

In loving memory of my father, and for all seniors who wish to celebrate their incredible journeys.

Inspired by Dr. Suess

You've gone many places, so far from your town.

You walked to your friend's house. You walked to the park.
You walked in the light, and played games in the dark.

You discovered the road trip which opened up doors.
Cities to cities and shores to shores.

You drove to the beach, then to the casino.
You drove in your best friend's blue El Camino.

OH, THE PLACES YOU'VE BEEN!

You flew to the islands. You flew to the lakes.
You flew to the jungles. Watch out for the snakes!

You flew to see buttes and cliffs galore.
Don't get me started on the Cliffs of Moher.

Each new destination you did embrace.

Bora, Bora was breathtaking, as was Machu Pichu.
But this glorious highest place will astound even you.

WONDERFUL Places I Traveled As An Adult

www.ingramcontent.com/pod-product-compliance
Lightning Source LLC
Chambersburg PA
CBHW041429080526

44579CB00021B/48